D0906752

oct. 20, 2017

The Seven Sacred Teachings
OF WHITE BUFFALO CALF WOMAN

Niizhwaaswi Aanike'iniwendiwin
WAABISHIKI MASHKODE BIZHIKIINS IKWE

David Bouchard & Dr. Joseph Martin
PAINTINGS BY Kristy Cameron
FLUTES AND MUSIC BY Swampfox
FOREWORD BY Dendreah
OJIBWE TRANSLATION BY Jason AND Nancy Jones

MORE THAN WORDS
MTW
PUBLISHERS

PREFACE
BY DAVID BOUCHARD

The Seven Sacred Teachings of White Buffalo Calf Woman, also known as the Seven Grandfather Teachings, are shared, valued and practised by many indigenous peoples.

These Teachings are universal; however, for the purpose and framework of this telling we have used many of the beliefs of the Ojibwe/Chippewa/Anishinaabe; that is, the colours of the Medicine Wheel, the direction of life's journey beginning in the east moving clockwise, and associating certain wildlife, plant and tree life with specific Teachings.

Rooted in humility and honesty, the creators of this book have tried to respect the cultures and traditions of all peoples.

It is our hope that this telling will unite and thus heal divisions. Prophecies tell that this is the time for One Heart, One Mind and One Drum. We, readers and authors alike, are the ones we have been waiting for. There is nobody else who can revitalize our culture and values except ourselves.

It is our hope that our telling might move readers toward greater courage and wisdom and ultimately toward achieving and understanding what is true in life's journey.

With all love,

Miigwech

Niizhwaaswi aanike'iniwendiwin gagiikwewin. Waabishiki Mashkode Bizhikiins ikwe. Aanike naamaadiiwag anishinaabeg gagiikwewin.

Gakinago awiya izhi-gikinoo'amawaa odaabijitoonaawaan aninishaabeg. Inashke awe mashkiki waawiyeyaatig gaa-inaaboowateg. Inashke waabinong gaabii-onji-waabang; gii-ani-giizhigak giizis gwayak gaa-izhaadizhaawin inashke ogowe gaye onowe gidiniwemaaganinaanig awesiinhyag giigoonhyag, binesiwag, mitagamig gaanitaawigingin.

Weweni gaamaajiigingin gaanisitawinamang, Ogowe gaagii-ozhitoowaad owe mazina'igan gakina endaswe-waanagiziyang weweni ji-nisidotaadiyang.

Inashke owe dibaajimowin mii'omaa ge-ondinamang, ji-okonoojimooyang. Ogowe gichi-anishinaabeg giwindamaagonaanig ningo-naanaagadawendamowin, ningode', dewe'igan. Gaa-agindaasoyang gaye gaa-ozhibii'igeyang, miiwag ogowe gaabaabii'angwaa apane. Gaawiin bekaanizid awiya odaa'aanjimokibidoosiin anishinaabemowinan gaye gagiikwewinan, giinawind gidaawimin.

Mii'awenake enaabishinang inendamangwaa ogowe gaa-agindaasowaad jide-apii-jide-'ewaad gaye ji-debweyenendizoyang gaye weweni ji-nisitodamang gwayako-naanaagadawendamowin gaye ezhichigewin.

Ginakoomininim

Miigwech

FOREWORD
BY WHITE BUFFALO CALF WOMAN
GIMAAMAA'INAAN GAYE GOOKOMISINAAN

Long ago, I heard my children cry.

Four days later, I took on the shape of a White Buffalo Calf. Four days after that, I went to them. And over the next four days, I taught them Sacred Songs and Dances and I taught them the Seven Sacred Ceremonies.

I taught them the Sun Dance. I taught them to Fast. I taught them the sacred and traditional ceremonies necessary for youth Coming of Age. I gifted them with the Peace Pipe and taught them how to use it. I taught them the ways of the Medicine Wheel. I taught them to seek their paths to The Good Red Road by reaching out to me through the Vision Quest. And I taught them how to build and use the Sweat Lodge.

Mewinzha ninijaanisag ningii-noondawaag mawiwaad.

Eko niiyogonigak ningii-izhinaago'idiz Waabishiki Mashkode Bizhikiins. Miinawaa eninii'ogonigak, ningii-ani-andawaabamaag niiyo'ogonidash minik ningii-gikinoo'amawaag, ningii-gikinoo'amawaag manidoonagamonan, gaye niimiwinan gaye niizhwaachi gagiikwewinan.

Ningii-gikinoo'amawaag giizisoshimowin. Ningii-gikinoo'amawaag jigii-igoshimowaad. Ningii-gikinoo'amawaag gagiikwewinan ogowe gaa-ani'ombigiwaad. Ningii-miinaag opwaaganan ningii-gikinoo'amawaag genaabaji'aawaad. Ningii-wiindamowaad enaabadak mashkiki waawiyeyaatig. Gikinoo'amawaag weweni ji-bima'adoowaad mino-miikana. Gagwe-gikendamowaad gwayakwendamowin. Gaye ningii-gikinoo'amawaag ji-onakidoowaad madoodison.

I told them that they were responsible for watching over the land, their four-legged brothers and All their Relations.

Today, I return as White Buffalo Calf Woman. Today, I return with Seven Sacred Teachings.

Open your minds and your hearts to Grandfather Universe, Father Sun, Grandmother Moon, Mother Earth and to all of the flyers, swimmers, walkers, crawlers, burrowers and standing ones. Accept the Teachings of Grandfather Rock, the elements, the colours and my Seven Sacred Dimensions. Be open to All Your Relations, so that through them you can walk your journey through life along The Good Red Road.

When you follow these Seven Sacred Teachings, you might then live in peace and harmony with All Your Relations.

The four directions of the Medicine Wheel represent the four colours of two-leggeds: Yellow (East), Red (South), Black (West) and White (North). There are three other directions; Up, Down and Within.

Ningii-inaag wiinawaa weweni ji-ganawendamowaad owe aki, gaye. Gaa-niiyogaadewaad, gaye gidinawemaagininaanig.

Noongom gibi'azhe giiweyaan Waabishiki Mashkode Bizhikiins nindaw. Noongom-nimbiidoonan niizhwaaching aanike gagiikwewinan.

Baakinan ginaanaagadawen-damiwiniwaan gaye gide'iwaan Gimishoomisinaan odibenjigewin, Gimishoomisinaan, Gookomisinaan, Gimaamaa'inaan, gakina endaswaa biminaagoziwaad gidinawemaaganinaanig. Odaapendan ogikinoo'amaagewinan gimishoomisaabikwanaan, gaa-izhiwebak, gaa-inaabootegin, niizhwaaswo aanike-gagiikwewinan. Baakendan ji-ani-oko mino-bimaa'adooyeg misko-miikana.

Giishpin biminizha'aman onowe niizhwaaswi aanike-gagiikwewinan. Giga-mino-bimaadiz wiiji'inenimadwaa gidinawemaaganag.

Niiwing endaso-ondaanimak waawiye-mashkikiiwaatig niwewaan gaa'inaabooteg inaabishkaagewaad gaa-niizhoogaadewaad.

Look to the Seven Directions and seek out which of your wild cousins best represents each Teaching. By studying nature, you can best understand yourself and these Teachings. And study shapes, colours and songs too. Open your heart as well as your eyes. My Teachings are waiting to be discovered.

Discover them, then teach them to your children. Share them with all those you love, and share them with your enemies too. You are all my children.

It was told that next time there is chaos and disparity, She would return again. She said She would return as a White Buffalo Calf. Some believe She already has.

WORDS OF CHIEF ARVOL LOOKING HORSE, 19TH GENERATION KEEPER OF THE SACRED WHITE BUFFALO CALF PIPE OF THE LAKOTA NATION

Iwedi inaabin niizhwaaching wendaanimak naanaagadawenim awenen a'aa naanaagadawaabam gidinawemaagan weweni Gaa-gikendaasod. Weweni naanaagajichigeyan, weweni giga-naanaagazotaadiz gaye onowe gagiikwewinan. Naanaagajitoon gaa-izhijiiyaagin, enaabootegin, gaye nagamonan. Baakinan gide' gaye gishkiinzhigoon. Ningikinoo'amaagoowinan mookishkaawan.

Mookinan gikinoo'amaw gininijaanisag. Maada'oosh ogowe gaa-zhawemadwaa ogowe gaye gaamaaneminikwaa. Giinawaa gakina ninijaanisag.

Giitabaajimom miinawaa wiipi azhe-giiwed ikwe. Gii-ikido wiipi-azhe-giiwed a'aa Waabishki Mashkode Bizhikiins. Aanind enedamoo giipi-azhe-giiwed.

WORDS OF CHIEF ARVOL LOOKING HORSE, 19TH GENERATION KEEPER OF THE SACRED WHITE BUFFALO CALF PIPE OF THE LAKOTA NATION

HUMILITY • DIBAADENDIZOWIN

Begin your journey in the spring, in the east. East is where all life begins and yellow best represents my first Teaching: Humility.

Every day, the beauty and power of creation are ignited in the east. Are you not humbled by the strength and brilliance of the rising sun? Can you not sense that there is something much stronger than you out there? Accept how small and insignificant you are. For the betterment of yourself and all Creation, strive to be humble.

Look to Wolf – Ma'iingan – for humility. Observe how Ma'iingan does not live for himself but for the pack. Watch him bow his head in the presence of others. He does this out of deference, not fright. Ma'iingan understands what a small part of the whole he plays. His ultimate punishment is to be cast away from his community.

Learn this kind of humility. Learn to not be arrogant. Do not think too highly of yourself. Do not want for yourself. Become Ma'iingan. Become humble.

Waabanong onji-maajitaan babaa-andawaabiiyan. Mii'iwedi waabanong baa'onjishkaag bimaadiziwin gaye gaa-bagakii-ozaawaag onjinaagwad nitam ningikinoo'amaagoowin: Dibaadendizowin

Endaso giizhik ishpendamowin bii-onji-ombakone waabanong. Gaawiin ina gidishpendanzii bimooko'ag gimishoomisinaan? Gaawiin ina giibiidamanjitoonsiin nawaj gegoo ishpendaagwak. Na'endan gidinaamaagenimoyan gaye agaasenimoyan. Nawaj jina'endaman epiitenimoyan.

Inashke ma'iingan ganawaabam epiitenimoyan. Inashke gaawiin eta gagwe-bimaaji'idizosii odapenimaa' wiiji-aya'aa'. Ganawaabam nanawagikwetaad niibawiitawaad wiiji-waawiidoopamaad. Ma'iingan onisidotaan bangii ezhichiged. Onaagajitoon bakeyaakonidiwin.

Gikendan owe apiitenimowin. Gikendan ji-ishpenimosiwan. Gego ishpenimizoken. Gego giineta inenindizoken. Naabenim ma'iinganinenimon.

Tobacco, Sage, Cedar and Sweetgrass are the four sacred plants. Of these, Tobacco is the most important. Always carry Tobacco with you so that you can offer it in thanks.

Now, find a quiet place under the tree that best represents humility; the Trembling Aspen. From its branch, make a flute and play me a song in C, as C is the key that is in tune with humility. Through this, I will recognize your gratitude and all will be good.

We all walk this Good Earth Road as creatures of the One Creator. The rising and falling of the Sun each day, the seasons, the gifts of food, shelter, love and friendship are there for each of us in the One Circle. If you cannot find the way to be grateful in your heart, the fault lies within you.

TECUMTHE, TECUMSEH

Asemaa, Nookwesigan, Giishkaandag, gaye Wiinbashk niiwin ishpendaago mashkiki. Onowe asemaa gichi-ishpendaagozi. Apanego gigizin asemaa.

Mikan ezhi-binaanak jiigazaad, maanizaatig. Wadikwaning onji-ozhitoon genagamwaageyan nagamitoon apiitenamowin. Mii'owe ji-nisidawinamaan gidapiitenamowin.

Gakina gibimi-'atoomin giinawind omaa gaagii-asinang mishoomisinaan. Endaso mooko'ang miinawaa bangishimong, izhiningo gikinoonowin, wiisiniwinan gaa-miinigoowiziyang, endaayang, zaagi'iiwewin, iwe zhaawenigewin ayaamagad aabiding gizhibaabiiyang. Giishpin mikanziwan, na'enimowin gide'ing, giin gibishigwendaan.

TECUMTHE, TECUMSEH

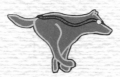

HONESTY • GWAYAKOWAADIZIWIN

Come summer, travel south, where the sun is at its highest. There, learn Honesty.

The sun is red hot and you are living your youth. This is the midday of your journey.

Now is the time for you to be honest with yourself; see and accept yourself for who you are. Then and only then might you accept others for who they are.

Be honest with yourself as well as with others. When you speak, speak truthfully.

Kitchi-Sabe is the four-legged who walks on two legs. Sabe reminds us to be ourselves and not someone we are not. An honest person is said to walk tall like Kitchi-Sabe.

Raven understands Honesty. Like Kitchi-Sabe, Raven accepts himself and knows how to use his gift. He does not seek the power, speed or beauty of others. He uses what he has been given to survive and thrive. So must you. To want more than you have been given is to suggest that the Creator has not given you enough. You have enough.

Niibin, zhaawanong izhaan, imaa gimishoomisinaan ishpa'ang. Mii'omaa ji-gakendaman gwayakwendamowin.

Gizhaasige gimishoomisinaan gidooshkibimaadiz. Mii'owe naawigiizhigad ginandawaabanjigewin.

Mii' izhigwa ji-gagwe-debweyenimoyan; waabandizon debweyendan. Mii'iw ji-debweyenimadwaa gewiinawaa.

Debwetaadizon gaye wiinawaa. Gaagiidoyan debweyan aabajitoon.

Gichi-misaabe niiyogaade niizho-bimosegaagenan okaadan. Misaabe gidigonaan ginawindigo jiiyaawiyang gaawiin awiya bekaanizid. Weweni gaa-inaadizid ginooziibimose daabishkoo misaabe.

Gaagaagi onisidotaan nibwaakaayendamowin. Daabishkoo misaabe, gaagaagi debweyenimo ogikendaanan enaabijitood omiinigoowizinan. Gaawiin awashime enimosii apiich gakina awiya odaabijitoon omiinigowiziwin ji-bimaadizid. Miigo gegiin bezhigwan. Nawaj andawendaman aazha dena'iminik gimiinig mandidoo.

Protect and ground yourself with Cedar. Then find a quiet place under the Cottonwood tree. From its branch, make a flute and play me a song in the key of D, for D is in tune with this Teaching of Honesty. I will hear your gratitude and all will be good.

Honesty comes when you learn to be fearless with yourself. When you speak and act straight from the heart, the Creator will give you love and strength to say and do what is right for you in every moment. Innocence, curiosity and openness will keep you honest.

GOYATHLAY, GERONIMO

Ganawenidizon Giishkaandag apagwana'odizon. Gagwemikan ezhibinaanak agwani adoopaatigong. Wadikwaning onji-ozhitoon ge-nagamwaageyan, gaabijitoon gwayakwaadizii gikinoo'aagewin. Giga-noondawin miigwechiwendaman.

Gwayakwaadiziwin onjimagad ji-zoongenindizoyan. Gii-gaagiigidoyan gide'ing onjisitoon manidoo giga-miinig gizhewaadiziwin jide-apiitendaman ikidoyan ezhichigeyan gaye apanego. Anishaawendam, ogagwe-waabandaan, gaye hagakendamowin giga-gwayakwaadiz.

GOYATHLAY, GERONIMO

RESPECT • MANAAJI'IWEWIN

In the fall, travel west.

The sun sets in the west as Turtle Island becomes black.

Look to Buffalo – Bashkode-bizhiki – for one who models Respect. And honour him. That Bashkode-bizhiki offers himself to sustain you does not make his life any less than yours. It makes it more.

Not long ago countless Bashkode-bizhiki roamed the west. I said that he would disappear if he was not respected. Is respect, like Bashkode-bizhiki, disappearing from Turtle Island?

Do not waste. Use all things wisely. Never take more than you need and always give away that which you do not use. And treat others as you would have them treat you, respectfully. Learn respect and learn balance. What goes up will come down. What you do for others will be done for you. What you give away will always come back to you in the One Circle.

Gii-dagwaagig ningaabii'inong izhaan.

Izhi-bangishimon ningaabii'anong mikinaakominis izhi-gashkii-dibikak.

Inashke waabam Mashkode Bizhiki gaanaagotood manaajii'itowin. Gaye gichi-apiitenim. A'aw Mashkode Bizhiki gidinenimigonaan ji-mino-bimaadiziyan. Bangiiyendaagozisii nawaj geyaabi.

Gaawiin aapiji mewinzha giikagenendaagoziwag ningaabii'anong. Ningii-ikid ji-angonaagozid giishpin manaajii'aasowin. Aniwanisin ina manaajii'itiwin ani-maajaamagad ina manaajii'itiwin mikinaakominising odaabishkoo Mashkode Bizhiki?

Gakina gegoo minwaabijitoon. Gego awashimc odaapinangen gaye apanego miigiwen gaa-andawendanziwan. Miigo bezhigwan gedoodawadwaa ezhi-andawendaman ji-doodawikwaa...gwayakwaadiziwin. Gikendan manaajii'itiwin gaye dibishkooshkwaawin. Gaa-ishpishkaag onjida dabinaazhikaa. Endoodawadwaa awiyag gewiinawaa giga-doodaagoog. Awegonen gaa-miigiweyan giga-bi-azhe-giiwenodaagon gizhibaa-ishkaag.

Burn Sage under Western Cedar. From its branch, make a flute and play me a song in the key of E. I will hear your gratitude and all will be good.

If you want to live in peace with All Our Relations, you will be able to do so when you treat all creatures alike with respect. Give them all the same kind consideration. Give them all an even chance to live and grow. All Our Relations were made by the same Great Spirit. We are all sisters and brothers, after all.

HINMATON YALATKIT, CHIEF JOSEPH

Nookwezigen Giishikikaan. Wadikwaning onji-ozhitoon ge-nagamwaageyan, nagamotawishin gaa-inweg iiiiiitaagwad. Ninga-noondaan gimiigwechiwendam gaye damino-ayaa.

Giishpin weweni wii-bimaadiziyan gakina gidinawemaaganinaanig miigo, ge-izhi-gashkijigeyan giishpin weweni inenamadwaa gaa-wiidanakiimangwaa gaye manaajii'itiwin. Miigo gakina naasaab apiitenim. Gakina inenim ji-ombigiwaad. Gakina gidinawemaaganinaanig manidoo gigii-izhi-ozhi'igonaan. Gakina giwiiji'ayaa'aawindamin

HINMATON YALATKIT, CHIEF JOSEPH

COURAGE • ZOONGIDE'EWIN

Go north in winter.

On northern white plain, you will come to understand how life moves from one world to the next.

Look to Bear – Makwa – to model Courage.

You are older now. Your hair is white. You are in the winter of your life. You have learned much. You understand to always act on what is right for you and for your family. To do what is right is not easy. It takes courage. It takes courage to heal that which is not well within you before being reborn. Become healer. Become Makwa.

Just as courage sleeps in Makwa through long winter months, it is dormant within you. It need only be awakened.

Observe Makwa fight when her young are threatened. She will not stop until she overcomes any and all threats. In your life, you will need courage to transform fears that might prevent you from living a good life. Makwa shows you how to face fear and danger.

Giiwedinong izhaan biboon.

Waabishki giiwedinong giga-ninisotaan ezhi-biijinishkaag owe bezhig miinawaa aandaki.

Inashke waabam makwa onaagotoon zoongendamowin.

Gigichi-ayaayaaw. Giwaabikwe. Biboonendaagwad gibimaadiziwin. Aazha niibowa gigikendaan. Ginisidotaan weweni gedoodaman giin gaye giwiigamaaganag. Gaawiin wendasinoon gagwe-gwayakochigewin. zoongide'ewin. Nawaj zoongide'ewin ji-noojimoomagak iwe gaa-onji-mino-ayaasiwan jibwaa- aanji nitaawigiiyan. Noojimo'iwen. Daabishkoo Makwa.

Giizhiibaangwashiiyang daabishkoo Makwa izhin ningo-biboon. Gaagigi ishkaagoyan. Andawendaagod goshkozimakad.

Inashke waabam gigizhaawasot. Gaawiin dagibijiisii baamaa gakina gii'amawaad. Gii-bimaadiziyan zoongide'en ji-mino-bimaadiziyan. Makwa giwaabanda'ig zegiziwin gaye naniizaanendamowin.

Sweetgrass is the hair of Mother Earth. Braid her hair before you cut it. Leave her an offering of Tobacco. Then find a quiet place under Northern Fir and make a flute in the key of G. I will hear your gratitude and all will be good.

Every struggle, whether won or lost, strengthens us for the next to come. It is not good for people to have an easy life. They become weak and inefficient when they cease to struggle. Some need a series of defeats before developing the strength and courage to win a victory.

VICTORIO

Wiinbashk odoowiinizisinan gimaamaanaan. Apikaazh jibwaa-giishkikonad. Biindaakoozh. Mikan ezhi-bizaanak anaami giiwedinozhingobaandag gaye. Wadikwaning onji-ozhitoon genagamwaageyan jiiiiigaa-initaagwak. Ninga-noondaan gimiigwechiwendam gaye damino-ayaa.

Endaso gagwejiiyan, maagizhaa niiwezhiweyan, maagizhaa gaye niiwenigooyan, mii'omaa wenji-mashkawendamang dibishkoo miinawaa naagaj. Gaawiin onishishizinoon ji-wendak bimaadiziwing. Ani-zhaagwaadiziwag gibichendamoog ji-zoongendamowaad. Aanind onandawenaawaa niibowa ji-zhaagoji'indwaa jibwaa-biidamanjitooyan mashkawendamowin.

VICTORIO

WISDOM • NIBWAAKAAWIN

You have traveled the way of the Medicine Wheel. Now, look up to the blue of Grandfather Sky for Wisdom.

To live your life based on your unique gift is to live wisely.

You are not the same as your neighbour. You were created special. You are one of a kind. So is your neighbour. So are the tree and the flower. You need only look to see that it is so. Do not ask questions. Watch and listen. Notice what is going on around you. Observe your life and the lives of others. By watching and listening you can learn everything you need to know. Knowledge can be learned. Wisdom must be lived. Live and learn.

Look into any clear lake. You do not see your reflection. You see that of those who came before you. Through All Your Relations and this Teaching of Wisdom, you will come to use your gift to direct your life's journey. Do not live based on what you wish you were. Live on what you are. If you have been given the gift of song, then sing. If yours is the gift of dance, then dance.

Gigii-pima'adoon iwe mashkikiiwaatig. Inaabin, giizhigong ezhi-ozhaawashkwagoodeg, gimishoomisinaan onibwaakaawin.

Ji-bimaadiziyan naagijitoon gimiini-goowiziwinan ji-mino-bimaadiziwin.

Gaawiin bezhigwan gidinaadizisii gaajiigidaamad. Weweni gigii-ozhii'igoo. Giin wa'awe bezhig. Miigo awe gaajiigidaamad. Gaye mitigoog miinawaa waabigwan. Inashke naabiyan gigikendaan. Gegoo memwech michi-naanaagadawaabin. Gaye, bizindan. Naanaagijitoon ezhiseg gegooyan. Naanaagijitoon gibimaadiziwin gaye igiwedi aanind. Giishpin naanaagidawaabiyan miinawaa bizindaman mii'omaa ge-onji-gikendaman gakina gegoo. Gikendamowin daagikendaagwad. Nibwaakaawin inaadizin. Inaadizin bagakendan.

Inaabin zaaga'igan gawaakamig. Gaawiin gii-waabandanziin gimazinaatebiigishinowin. Gii-waabandaan igiwe aazha gaapime ayaawaad. Gakina gidiniwemaaganag o'owe nibwaakaagewin. Gigayaabijitooyan gimiinigoowiziwinan ji-gwayak-goshkaag ji-ani-bimaadiziyan. Gego wiin apane andawendagen gaa-inaadizisiwan. Bizaan weweni bimaadizin. Giishpin gimiinigowiziyan nagomonan, nagamon. Giishipin niimiigowiziyan niimiwin, niimin.

Look to Beaver – Amik – for Wisdom. Amik has formidable teeth. Do you know what will become of Amik if he does not use his gift? His teeth will grow until they are no longer of any use to him. They will hinder him. Amik uses his gift wisely to thrive and so must you.

Now is the time to ponder over life, death and rebirth. And be grateful for the gift you have been given in this life.

Feed on Corn, the first of the Three Sisters. Then find a Poplar tree and from the branch of this Standing One whose arms reach high into blue sky, make a flute in the key of F. I will hear your gratitude and all will be good.

Open to the kindness, quiet, silence and gentleness inside your own heart, for it is here when you quietly tune to Mother Earth that you can hear Her voice. You can hear Her beautiful songs of love that She sings to her minerals and crystal children. Hear the beautiful ballads and mystical plaintive chants that She sings to Her waters, earth, air, fire, ether, and the great strong healing remedy melodies that She sings to all Her bereaved and sickened animals who long for and need Her loving chants and melodies. You can hear Her also in the sighing winds as She cries for Her own creatures and children, including you.

TATANKA YOTANKA, SITTING BULL

Inashke ganawaabam amik onji-nibwaa-kaawin. Inashke giniin jiikaabide. Gigikendaan ina gezhiwebizipan amik aabijitoosig omiinigoowiziwinan? Daamaajii gininiwan wiibadan biinishigo gaawiin gegoo oganaabijitoosiinan. Gaawiin ogawiiji'isiinan. Weweni odaabijitoon omiinigoowiziwinan ji-bimaadizid.

Mii-izhigwa giibagamishkaag naanaagadewendaman aandakiiwin miinawaa oshi-nitaawigiwin. Gichi apiitendan gimiinigoowiziwinan owe bimaadiziwin.

Asham maadaaminag niswi ikwe wiiji'ayaag. Mikaw azaadi gaa-ginoowaadikwanimwid zaamishkang giizhik. Wadikwaning onji-ozhitoon ge-nagamwaageyan ef gaa-initaagwak. Ninga-noondaan gimiigwechiwendam gaye damino-ayaa.

Baakinan mino-ayaawin, ezhibizaanak, gaye bekaago gibiinjige'ing. Mii'i omaa ji-noondawaad gimaamaanaan. Ginoondaanan ozaazegaa nagamonan nagamowaad waakeyaasinii. Noondan ominotaagoziwin imaa nibikaang, ishpimiing, miinawaa ishkodeng, onagamonan onoojimo ishkaagonaawaan awesiinhyag. Awesiinhyag gaa-andawendamowaad nagomonan. Gidaa-noondaananigo gii-madweyaanimak nagomo'aad gakina odinawemaagana' gaye abinoojiinya' gaye giinigo.

TATANKA YOTANKA, SITTING BULL

TRUTH • DEBWEWIN

Truth is to know all these Teachings.

Look down toward the green earth. Everything comes from Mother Earth. Everything returns to Her.

Truth lies in spirit. Pray, every day. And when you can, pray under a tree, at sunrise if possible. Ask for yourself only when there is no other recourse. And give thanks, always. Give thanks with Tobacco. When you are thankful, good will come to you and to those you love.

Mother Earth was created on the back of Turtle – Miskwaadesii. Look to Miskwaadesii to understand truth.

There are thirteen Moons on her back; one for each moon cycle of one earth revolution around the sun. The Thirteen Moons and the Thirteen Grandmothers are signs that Mother Earth cares for you.

Look to Miskwaadesii for one whose existence is strong and stable. Slow-moving Miskwaadesii understands, as you should, that the journey of life is as important as the destination.

Debwewining onji-gikendan gagiikwewinan.

Inashke inaabin ozhaawashkwaa-aki. Gakina gegoo onjimagad gimaamaanaang. Gaye odazhegiiwe nodaagon.

Debwewining izhi-bimaadiziwin. Biindaakoonjigen endaso giizhik. Izhi-biindaakoonjigen jiigaatig jibwaa-mooko'ang giishpin gashkitooyan. Giinetogo dazhindazon. Apanego miigwechiwendan. Aapiji gidasemaa miigwechiwitaagoziyan. Miigwechiwendaman, minochigewin giga-debinaan ogowe gaye gaa-zhawenimadwaa.

Gimaamaanaan gii-onji-ozhichigaazo miskwaadesi opikwanaang. Ganawaabam Miskwaadesi ji-nisidotaman debwewin.

Midaaswaashi nisiwag giizisoog imaa opikwanaang. Endaso giizis aabiding giizhibaashkaa. Midaaswaashi niswi giizisoog okomisimaag mii'omaa wenji-naagwak zhaawenimik gimaamaanaan.

Ganawaabam miskwaadesi epiichi mashkawizid. Gaabesikaad miskwaadesi nisidotam, idash gaye giin, bimiiwidooyan gibimaadiziwin gichi-apiitendaagwad ezhi-ishkwesing.

Feed on Beans, the second of the Three Sisters. Then find an Oak tree. You can rely on the powerful Oak to always be there as a sign of my word to you. From its branch, make a flute and play me a song in A, the key of Truth. I will hear your gratitude and all will be good.

The Great Law of Peace from the Great Spirit is perfect, balanced, true and just in every way. Only when each person has the Living Laws of Peace within their heart, thoughts, words and actions will there be lasting peace among the Nations of the Earth.

DEGANAWIDEH, THE PEACEMAKER

Asham omashkoziisimina' aanike niswi ikwe wiiji'ayaag. Mikaw mitogomizh. Gida-inenimaa mitigomizh apane imaa ji-ayaad gaagii-ininaan. Wadikwaning onji-ozhitoon ge-nagamwaageyan eh gaa-initaagwak. Ninga-noondaan gimiigwechiwendam gaye da-mino-ayaa. Noondaagomoochiganens ef gaa-initwaagwak.

Gichi-inaakonigewin minochigewin gichi-manidoo gichendaagozi gaye debwewaadizi izhi-gakina gegoo. Endaso bezhigoyang gidabiitaamin mino'de'ewin, inendamowin, ikidowinan, gaye izhichigewinan. Da-ayaamagad minochigewin omaa gidakiiminaang.

DEGANAWIDEH, THE PEACEMAKER

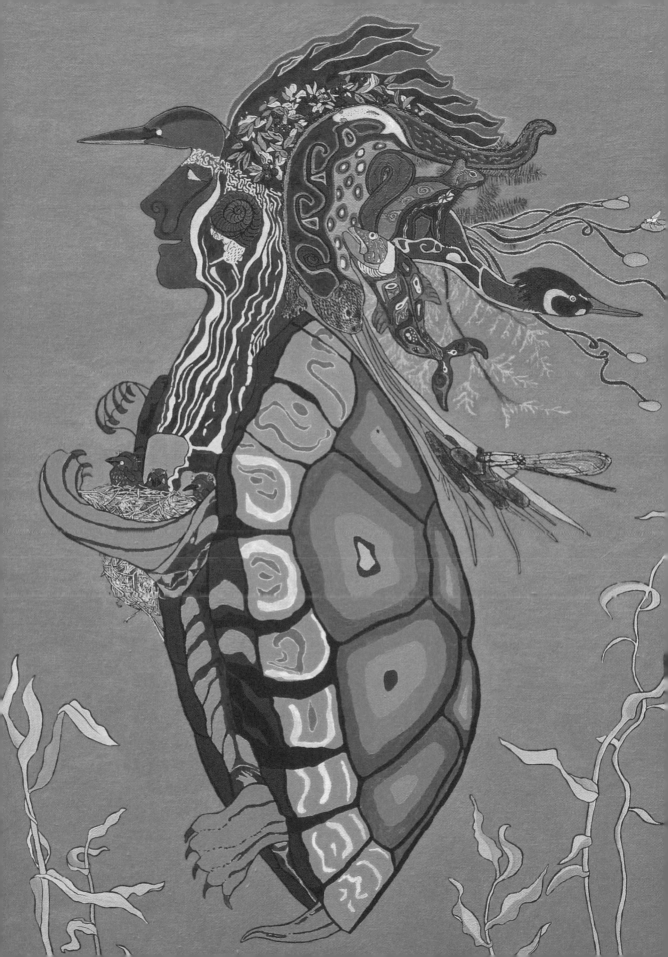

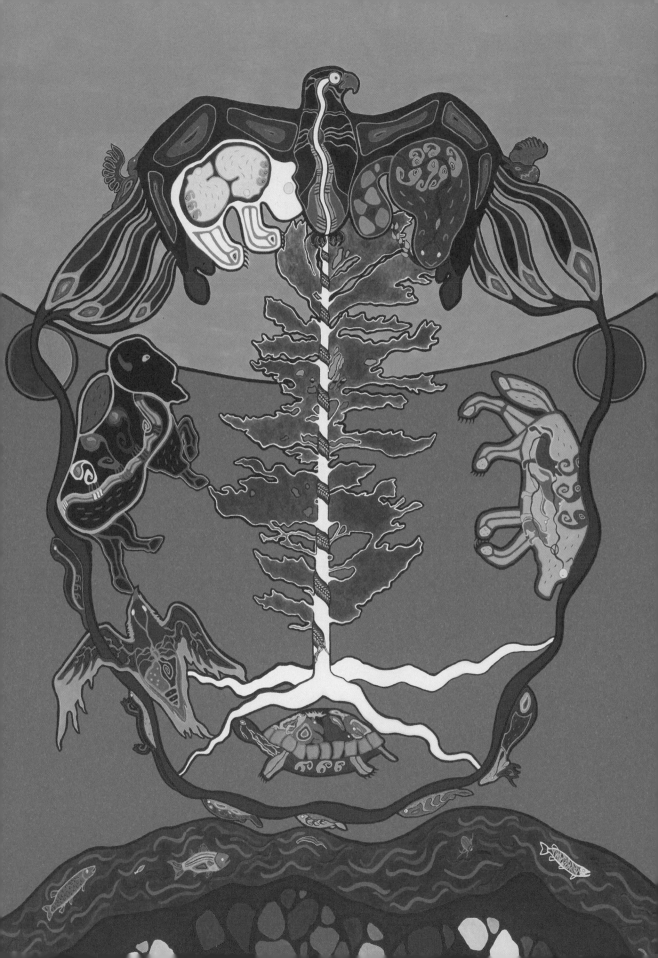

LOVE • ZAAGI'IDIWIN

Look within yourself for Love. Love yourself, and then love others.

You cannot love another until you first learn to love yourself.

You must understand and live the other six Teachings before you can love.

Love is worth working for. Love is worth waiting for. Love is the key to life.

There is no short cut to achieving the state of love and you cannot know love unless you are courageous. You cannot know love unless you are honest. Love is based on the wisdom to understand one's self and the humility to accept weaknesses as well as being proud of one's strengths. Love has as its very core the other Teachings. This is why I give it to you last.

The loving heart centre of each Uhkwehu:weh or true-hearted person lies within each of us.

Ganawaabandizon zhawenigewining, awiyag.

Gaawiin gidaa-zhawenimaasii awiya baamaa giishawenidizoyan.

Onjida ji-nisidotaman aanind ningodwaaswi gagiikwewinan jibwaa-zhawenjigeyan.

Gidaa-anokiitaan zhawenjigewin. Gidaa-baabiitoon zhawenjigewin. Zhawenjigwe mino-bimaadiziwin.

Gaawiin wiikaa gidaa-wiimaashkaziin gizhewaadiziwin gaye. Gaawiin gigakendanziin gizhewaadiziwin zoongendaman. Gaawiin gigakendanziin gizhewaadiziwin gwayakwaadiziyan. Gizhewaadiziwin ayaa gwayakwendamowining weweni ji-nisidotaadizoyan gaye. Inaadiziwin ji-nisidawinaman zhaagwaadiziwinan gaye gichi-apiitenidizoyan. Gizhewaadiziwin naawisin gagiikwewinan. Mii'owe gaagii-onji-miininaan iskwaaj.

Gaabizhiwaadizide'e gidizhibimiwidaasomin.

Love is deep violet and is modeled by Eagle – Migizi. Migizi flies high above the earth and sees all that is true. Migizi is honest. She is courageous. She exemplifies all my Teachings. She is closer to me than any other. Look to her as one who represents and models Love. And honour her, always.

Feed on the third sister, Squash. From the Tree of Peace, the White Pine, make a flute and play me a song in B, as B holds the key to My heart. I will be listening. I will hear your gratitude and all will be good.

I have been called The Greatest Warrior among All Our Relations. This may be so. What I learned to conquer were the challenges to my Heart Unity within my chest. Self-confidence and love strengthen everything inside you. This you can also do, my sister and brother. This is the time to continue your Good Red Road Journey, while still in the body.

TASHUNKE WITKO, CRAZY HORSE

Gizhewaadiziwin miinaabowate ogii-naagotoon migizi. Waasa ishpiming babaamaashi gakina owaabandaan gegoo debwewinan. Migizi gwayakwaadizi. Zoongendam. Mii'awe ogikinoo'aagewinan. Aapiji nimbeshwenimaa apiich baakaan awiya. Inashke ganawaabam mii'awe gaa-onendang gizhewaadiziwin. Apane gidaa-miigwechiwenimaa

Asham gichi-agoosimaan wiiji'ayaakweg ekoniswi. Gizhewaadiziizhingwaak. Wadikwaning onji-ozhitoon noondaagamoochiganens. Nagamotawishin biiii enitaagwad. Giga-bizindawin. Ninga-noondaan gimiigwechiwendamowin gaye mino-ayaawin.

Gichi-ogichidaa nindigoog gakina nindinawemaaganag. Maagizhaa geget. Ningii-gashkitoonan jibaajizikamaan onowe ninde'ing gaa-ayaagin. Ningii-tebweyenindiz gaye gizhewaadiziwin mii'iwe mashkawenindizoyan. Gegiinigo gidaa-gashkitoon nimisenh gaye nisayenh. Mii'opii ge-ani-maajii-andoyanban. Misko-miikana, megwaa bimiwidooyan giiyaw.

TASHUNKE WITKO, CRAZY HORSE

SEVEN SACRED TEACHINGS
NIIZHWAASWI AANIKE'INIWENDIWIN

My Teachings are not new.

The way I would have you live is essential so all may prosper and be happy. All you have to do is open your heart and listen. Understand My Teachings. Live by them.

Each Teaching exists in every one of My creations.

Every four-legged has something of Me. Every plant, every flower and every tree has something of Me. Every shape, size and colour has something of Me.

Look for them in all you see, in everything you are. Recognize and honour them.

And be grateful. Be thankful. It is good to give thanks.

Gaawiin oshki-ayaa'awizinoon onowe gaa-gikinoo'amawinaan

O'owe gaa-gikinoo'amawinaan mino-bimaadiziwin. Mii'etago ge-izhichigeyanban. Gide' aabijitoon bizindaman. Nisidotan gaa-gikinoo'amawinaan Mii'owe inaadiziyan.

Gakina gegoo naagwadoon onowe gakina gegoo gaagii-ozhisitooyaan.

Endaso niiyogaaded gegoo niinonji. Gakina gegoo gitigaanensan, mitigoog, gaye waabigwaniin odayaanaawaan gaagii-ozhisitooyaan. Gakina gaa-izhijiiyaagin, enigokwaagin, enaabootegin gakina gegoo gaagii-ozhisitooyaan.

Andawaabin giga-waabandaan enaadiziyan.

Nisidawinan gaye gichi-apiitendan. Gichi-apiitendan. Gidaa-miigwechiwendan. Onizhishin miigwechiwitaagozing.